PETER RABBIT™

Little
Learning
Book

BASED ON THE ORIGINAL AND AUTHORIZED STORIES
BY BEATRIX POTTER

F. WARNE & CO

1 2 3

How many can you count?

How many little rabbits,
eating radishes?

"First he ate some lettuces and some French beans,
and then he ate some radishes."

From *The Tale of Peter Rabbit*

How many yellow stockings,
for Sally Henny-penny?

"Oh, that's a pair of stockings belonging
to Sally Henny-penny."

From *The Tale of Mrs. Tiggy-Winkle*

3

How many kittens,
playing in the dust?

"Once upon a time, there were three little kittens,
and their names were Mittens, Tom Kitten and Moppet."
From *The Tale of Tom Kitten*

4

How many guinea-pigs,
going gardening?

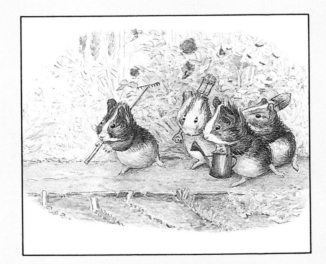

"We have a little garden,
A garden of our own,
And every day we water there
The seeds that we have sown."

From *Cecily Parsley's Nursery Rhymes*

5

How many mice,
snippeting and snappeting?

"There was a snippeting of scissors, and a snappeting of thread;
and little mouse voices sang loudly and gaily."

From *The Tailor of Gloucester*

6

How many fat Flopsy Bunnies?

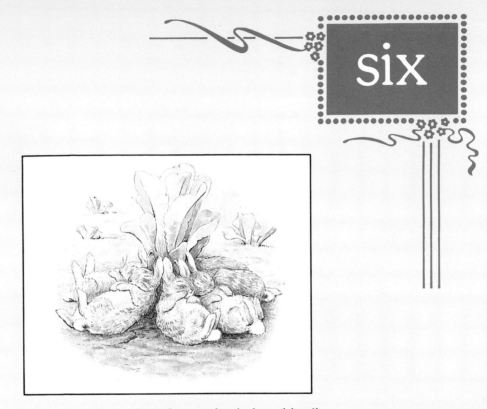

" 'One, two, three, four, five, six leetle fat rabbits!'
repeated Mr. McGregor, counting on his fingers."
From *The Tale of The Flopsy Bunnies*

7

How many red squirrels,
with the old brown owl?

"Nutkin danced up and down like a *sunbeam*,
but still Old Brown said nothing at all."

From *The Tale of Squirrel Nutkin*

8

How many piglets,
feeding from a trough?

eight

"Four little boy pigs and four little girl pigs
are too many altogether."

From *The Tale of Pigling Bland*

9

How many mice
round the supper table?

nine

"The dinner was of eight courses;
not much of anything, but truly elegant."

From *The Tale of Johnny Town-Mouse*

How many mice,
living in the shoe?

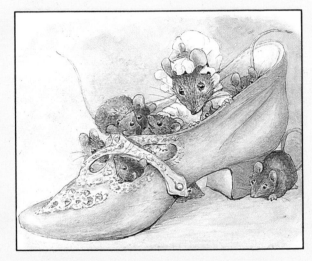

"I think if she lived in a little shoe-house –
That little old woman was surely a mouse!"
From *Appley Dapply's Nursery Rhymes*

11

How many birds
in the hen coop?

"The owner came with a lantern and a hamper
to catch six fowls to take to market in the morning."
From *The Tale of Pigling Bland*

12

How many animals
round the notice-board?

Endpaper design

How many rabbits can you see?

How many squirrels can you see?

How many mice can you see?

"Once upon a time there was a village shop.
The name over the window was 'Ginger and Pickles'."

From *The Tale of Ginger and Pickles*

How many shop-keepers
behind the counter?

How many customers
in front of the counter?

"The counter inside was a convenient height for rabbits."

From *The Tale of Ginger and Pickles*

How many rats inside the meal sack?

How many rats outside the meal sack?

Endpaper design for *The Tale of Samuel Whiskers*

A is for...?

Aa

a is for apples

"Cecily Parsley brewed good cider (from apples)."

Unpublished picture for *Cecily Parsley's Nursery Rhymes*

b is for butter

"Ribby went out down the field to the farm,
to fetch some milk and butter."

From *The Tale of The Pie and The Patty-Pan*

Cc

c is for carrot

Cc

"This is a nice gentle Rabbit.
His mother has given him a carrot."

From *The Story of A Fierce Bad Rabbit*

Dd

d is for ducks

Dd

"The three Puddle-ducks came along the hard
high road, marching one behind the other."

From *The Tale of Tom Kitten*

E e

e is for eggs

"Eggs, new-laid! Fresh new-laid eggs!"

From *The Tale of Little Pig Robinson*

Ff

f is for flowers

"'How do you do, my dear Ribby?' said Duchess.
'I've brought you some flowers.'"

From *The Tale of The Pie and The Patty-Pan*

Gg

g is for gate

"Peter, who was very naughty, ran straight away
to Mr. McGregor's garden, and squeezed under the gate!"

From *The Tale of Peter Rabbit*

H h

h is for ham

Hh

"Tom Thumb set to work at
once to carve the ham."

From *The Tale of Two Bad Mice*

Ii

i is for ink

" Dr. Maggotty was occupied
in putting rusty nails into a bottle of ink."

From *The Tale of The Pie and The Patty-Pan*

Jj

j is for jacket

"Mr. McGregor hung up the little jacket and
the shoes for a scare-crow."

From *The Tale of Peter Rabbit*

k is for kittens

"Once upon a time, there were three little kittens,
and their names were Mittens, Tom Kitten and Moppet."

From *The Tale of Tom Kitten*

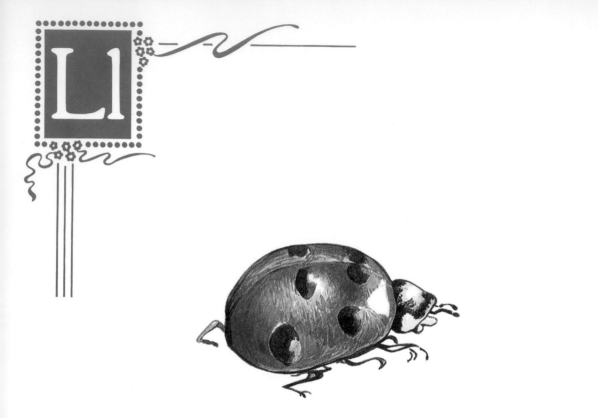

l is for ladybird

Ll

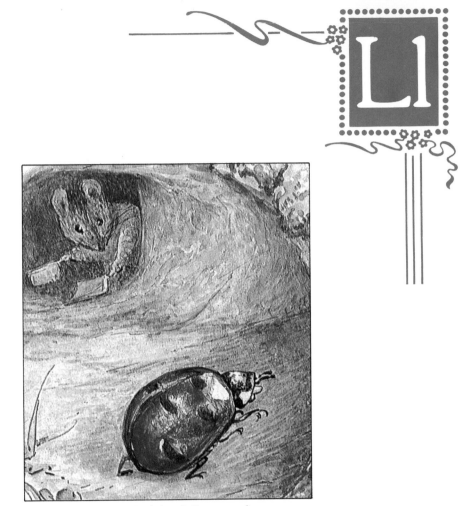

" 'Ladybird, ladybird, fly away home,
Your house is on fire and your children all gone' "
From *The Tale of Mrs. Tittlemouse* and *Beatrix Potter's Nursery Rhyme Book*

Mm

m is for mouse

Mm

"The mouse watches Miss Moppet
from the top of the cupboard."
From *The Story of Miss Moppet*

Nn

n is for newspaper

Nn

"Seated upon a stump, she was startled to find
an elegantly-dressed gentleman, reading a newspaper."

From *The Tale of Jemima Puddle-Duck*

o is for oranges

"There were two red lobsters and a ham, a fish,
a pudding, and some pears and oranges."

From *The Tale of Two Bad Mice*

Pp

p is for pigs

Pp

"And the other two little boy pigs,
Pigling Bland and Alexander, went to market."

From *The Tale of Pigling Bland*

q is for quilt

Qq

"Hunca Munca has got the cradle (and a quilt)
and some of Lucinda's clothes."

From *The Tale of Two Bad Mice*

Rr

r is for rabbits

"'One, two, three, four! five! six leetle rabbits!'
said he as he dropped them into his sack."

From *The Tale of The Flopsy Bunnies*

Ss

s is for strawberry

Ss

"Timmy Willie had been reared on roots and salad
(and sometimes a strawberry)."

From *The Tale of Johnny Town-Mouse*

T t

t is for tea-cup

Uu

Illustration by Beatrix Potter for *A Happy Pair*, by F. Weatherley

u is for umbrella

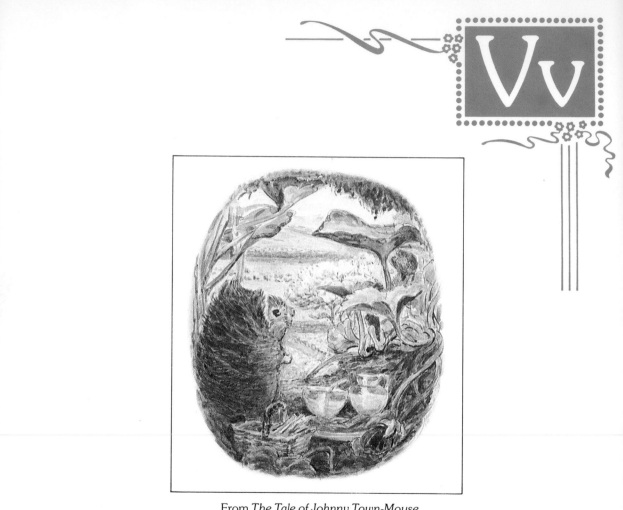

From *The Tale of Johnny Town-Mouse*

v is for violets

Ww

From *The Tale of Mrs. Tiggy-Winkle*

w is for washing

From *The Tale of Jemima Puddle-Duck*

x is in fox

Yy

From *The Tale of Mrs. Tiggy-Winkle*

y is for yard

From *The Tale of Mrs. Tittlemouse*

z is for "Zzz, bizz!"

Peter Rabbit's jacket is...?

blue?

red?

yellow?

blue

Peter Rabbit's jacket
is **blue**

"It was a blue jacket with brass buttons, quite new."
From *The Tale of Peter Rabbit*

red

Flopsy, Mopsy and Cotton-tail's
cloaks are **red**

"Flopsy, Mopsy, and Cotton-tail, who were good little bunnies, went down the lane to gather blackberries."
From *The Tale of Peter Rabbit*

Sally Henny-penny's stockings
are **yellow**

"That's a pair of stockings belonging to Sally Henny-penny –
look how she's worn the heels out with scratching in the yard."

From *The Tale of Mrs. Tiggy-Winkle*

Samuel Whiskers' coat
is **green**

"Mother, Mother!" said Mittens, "there has been an old man
rat in the dairy – a dreadful 'normous big rat."
From *The Tale of Samuel Whiskers*

purple

Tabitha Twitchit's dress
is **purple**

purple

"One day Mrs. Tabitha Twitchit expected friends to tea;
so she fetched the kittens indoors, to wash and dress them."

From *The Tale of Tom Kitten*

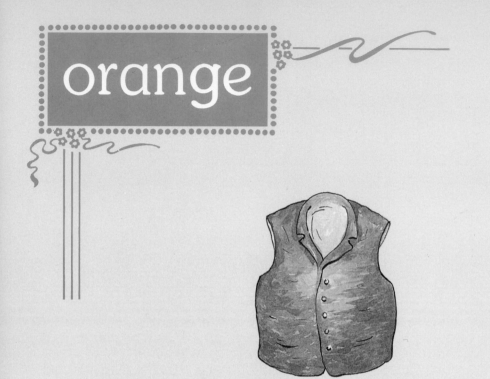

orange

Tommy Brock's waistcoat
is **orange**

orange

"Tommy Brock's clothes were very dirty; and as he slept
in the day-time, he always went to bed in his boots."

From *The Tale of Mr. Tod*

brown

Peter Rabbit's shoes
are **brown**

"It was the second little jacket and pair of shoes
that Peter had lost in a fortnight."

From *The Tale of Peter Rabbit*

pink

Miss Moppet's bow
is **pink**

"This is a Pussy called Miss Moppet,
she thinks she has heard a mouse!"
From *The Story of Miss Moppet*

turquoise

Old Mrs. Mouse's shoe
is **turquoise**

"You know the old woman
who lived in a shoe?"
From *Appley Dapply's Nursery Rhymes*

grey

The gentlemen rabbits' hats
are **grey**

grey

Two gentlemen rabbits walking in the snow.
From *Appley Dapply's Nursery Rhymes*

black

Sir Isaac Newton's waistcoat
is **black** and gold

gold

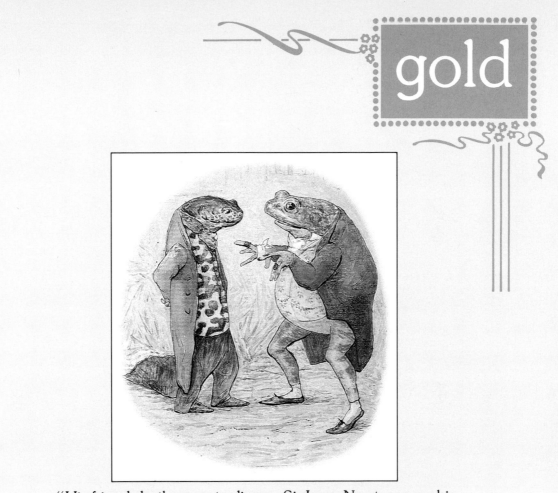

"His friends both came to dinner. Sir Isaac Newton wore his black and gold waistcoat."

From *The Tale of Mr. Jeremy Fisher*

Peter Rabbit's mother's
pocket-handkerchief
is **red** and white

white

"Peter was sitting by himself. He looked poorly,
and was dressed in a red cotton pocket-handkerchief."

From *The Tale of Peter Rabbit*

blue

Jemima Puddle-duck's shawl
is **blue** and **pink**

"She set off on a fine spring afternoon.
She was wearing a shawl and a poke bonnet."
From *The Tale of Jemima Puddle-Duck*

"Now I've finished my ironing: I'm going to air some clothes."
From *The Tale of Mrs. Tiggy-Winkle*

Mrs. Tiggy-Winkle washes and irons
all the animals' clothes.

"And she hung up all sorts and sizes of clothes."
From *The Tale of Mrs Tiggy-Winkle*

Then she hangs them up to air.

What time is it?

What time is it?

7 o'clock

Time for a wash
with Moppet

"First she scrubbed their faces
(this one is Moppet)."

From *The Tale of Tom Kitten*

What time is it?

8 o'clock

Time for breakfast
with Tommy Brock

"Tommy Brock was sitting at Mr. Tod's kitchen table,
pouring out tea from Mr. Tod's tea-pot."

From *The Tale of Mr. Tod*

What time is it?

9 o'clock

Time for tidying up
with Pigling Bland

"Pigling washed up the porridge plates in the bucket.
He sang while he worked."

From *The Tale of Pigling Bland*

What time is it?

10 o'clock

Time for a walk
with Timmy Willie

"And when the sun comes out again,
you should see my garden and the flowers."

From *The Tale of Johnny Town-Mouse*

What time is it?

11 o'clock

Time for a snack
with Mr. Jeremy Fisher

"I will eat a butterfly sandwich and
wait till the shower is over."
From *The Tale of Mr. Jeremy Fisher*

What time is it?

12 o'clock

Time for a boat ride
with Squirrel Nutkin

"They made little rafts out of twigs,
and they paddled away over the water."
From *The Tale of Squirrel Nutkin*

What time is it?

1 o'clock

Time for lunch
with Mrs. Tittlemouse

"Mr. Jackson sat such a while that he had to be asked
if he would take some dinner?"

From *The Tale of Mrs. Tittlemouse*

What time is it?

2 o'clock

Time for a nap
with the Flopsy Bunnies

"The little Flopsy Bunnies slept delightfully
in the warm sun."

From *The Tale of The Flopsy Bunnies*

What time is it?

3 o'clock
Time for shopping
with Mrs. Tiggy-winkle

"The customer says she will pay another time.
And Pickles makes a low bow and says, 'With pleasure, madam.'"
From *The Tale of Ginger and Pickles*

What time is it?

4 o'clock

Time for tea
with Ribby and Duchess

"The pie proved extremely toothsome,
and the muffins light and hot."

From *The Tale of The Pie and The Patty-Pan*

What time is it?

5 o'clock

Time for a game

with Tom Kitten

"There were very extraordinary noises over-head,
which disturbed the dignity and repose of the tea party."

From *The Tale of Tom Kitten*

What time is it?

6 o'clock

Time for cooking
with Mrs. Rabbit

"Peter's mother was busy cooking;
she wondered what he had done with his clothes."
From *The Tale of Peter Rabbit*

What time is it?

7 o'clock

Time for supper
with Flopsy, Mopsy and Cotton-tail

"Flopsy, Mopsy and Cotton-tail had bread and milk
and blackberries for supper."

From *The Tale of Peter Rabbit*

What time is it?

8 o'clock

Time for bed
with Peter Rabbit

"His mother put him to bed, and made some camomile tea;
and she gave a dose of it to Peter!"
From *The Tale of Peter Rabbit*

Oh no, what time is it,
Peter Rabbit?

FREDERICK WARNE

Published by the Penguin Group
Penguin Books Ltd, 80 Strand, London WC2R ORL, England
Penguin Putnam Inc., 375 Hudson Street, New York, N.Y. 10014, USA
Penguin Books Canada Ltd, 10 Alcorn Avenue, Toronto, Ontario, Canada M4V 3B2
Penguin Books (NZ) Ltd, Cnr Rosedale and Airborne Roads, Albany, Auckland, New Zealand
Penguin Books India (P) Ltd, 11 Community Centre, Panchsheel Park, New Delhi 110 017, India
Penguin Books (South Africa) (Pty) Ltd, 5 Watkins Street, Denver Ext 4, Johannesburg 2094, South
Africa

Penguin Books Ltd, Registered Offices: Harmondsworth, Middlesex, England

Visit our web site at: www.peterrabbit.com

First published by Frederick Warne as four separate titles 1987
This edition first published 2001
1 3 5 7 9 10 8 6 4 2

ISBN 07232 47935

Additional artwork by Colin Twinn

Printed and bound in Singapore by Tien Wah Press (Pte) Ltd